"You've got Parkinson's, but con: unlike all of the other neurologic you, it'll just make your life mise, diagnosed, by an expert.

Well, he got the first bit right, I do have Parkinson's. The bit in the middle is up for debate, since the medical profession keep on changing their minds (it might kill me) but the third part was totally wrong. Looking on the bright side my glass is always half full, mostly because of my tremor.

This book is a collection of humorous and thought-provoking poems about Parkinson's and the world in general as we came out of the pandemic and got our lives back.

"Love his poems."
Catherine M

"Really makes me laugh, please write more."
Diane M

"Not your average highfalutin stuff, really down to earth."
David G

"Mark has a poem for almost everything."
Andy H

"Can't poke too much fun at Parkinson's".
Mark

Mark was the first person with Parkinson's that I met after joining the charity earlier this year. His straightforward down-to-earth approach to living with the condition was remarkable, and his commitment to his poetry even more so!

I've seen in person the impact that these verses can bring to people close to Parkinson's and those who know little or nothing of the condition. It can span from laughter to tears - often in the same verse!

It is fantastic to see that he is continuing to write and express himself across such a range of topics and that this continues to be such a big part of his life.

James Jopling
Scotland Director
Parkinson's UK

Acknowledgements

Thanks to:

Charles Small for editing the book and giving me support and encouragement.

Tom C. Murray OBE for his excellent illustrations as always.

Forth Ports Limited, my employer before I retired early (due to ill health), for their generous donation, which helped to get this book produced and ensured that the profits were maximised for the charity.

Life's Per – Verse With Parkinson's

Mark Coxe

Mark Coxe Publishing
A Homemade Book

Dedicated to helping people treat Parkinson's with the contempt it deserves.

Dear Reader,

This is my second book of poetry and as usual I'm cocking a snook at Parkinson's, world events and life in general.

Personally, I still find some types of poetry overbearing and pretentious and if you feel that way too, you'll love my book.

My poems rhyme and most of them are gloriously disrespectful, so if you are easily offended close the book and put it down NOW!

My poetry has evolved since writing the first book and (even though I do say so myself) this collection is much better. If you enjoyed Reflections, you'll find this one much more entertaining.

All profits from the sale of this book will go to Parkinson's UK Scotland and to my local Parkinson's Support Group in Fife.

All the best,

(Parkey) Mark Coxe

Contents

Well, What D'Ya Know?

I have something that's called Parkinson's
What does that mean to you?
Well, probably not very much at all
But please continue, read on through.

For Parkinson's there is no cure
If you've got it, they can't fix it
Even though it is incurable
Don't mean you're a broken biscuit.

I'd like to try and change your view
On how Parkinson's is regarded
Are we an asset to society
Or should we all just be discarded?

In the modern world we live in
If it's broke it's thrown away
Well, some people who have Parkinson's
Get that feeling every day.

With my tremor and my shuffling gait
It might seem I'm not quite right
But if you'd a knife and I'd a gun
I could still beat you in a fight.

Continued

Now the gun was just a metaphor
I'm not seeking confrontation
My weapon, it is just a pen
The cornerstone of education.

I'd like to teach you folks out there
What it's like to be like me
Someone living with their Parkinson's
Someone you don't have to be.

So, this is what I'm going to do
I'm going to hold my head up high
Even though I might be broken
I'll do my best before I die.

How to help you change your attitude?
Probably not by writing verse
But I think you'll find that's not quite true
And the outcome's quite perverse.

Just think, while you've been reading this
You might find yourself surprised
Perhaps your attitude to Parkinson's
Has changed before your very eyes.

Volunteering

'Never volunteer for anything'
My dad once said to me
'You don't know where it'll take you'
That was his philosophy.

I'm glad I didn't pay dad heed
Volunteering's an addiction
To do your best and try to help
People fighting our affliction.

So why become a volunteer
What has made me want to help?
To volunteer, with all I've got
To give my Parkinson's a skelp.

Perhaps it's simply comradeship
So many people now my friend
Suppose I'm grateful to you, Parkinson's
Although you drive me round the bend!

A Positive Thing About Parkinson's

If we were overrun by zombies
Having Parkinson's, you'd be safe
You'd blend in with all the living dead
And shuffle safely around the place.

Because without your medication
Since the pharmacy is closed
You'd end up looking like a zombie
Except that zombies decompose.

On Days Like These

The opening sequence of the Italian Job,
Sung by Matt Monro, that crooning heartthrob.

The 'union-flag' Minis racing round and around,
While the music blares out, makes a glorious sound.

Great Britain performing at its very best,
Making 'Foreign Johnnies' look completely inept.

Lovely Lorna, please go 'Just get on the plane',
Now the Mafioso has entered the frame.

The Mafia Boss makes a 'dig' at the car,
"You're only supposed to blow the bloody doors off!"
(Best film line by far.)

Strange Professor Peach on the floor with Annette!
"They went that-a-way" and the job's a success.

The Dormobile guys celebrating the match,
The Turin Police just don't know who to catch.

Continued

Two 'Nine Bob Notes' Mr Bridger and 'Camp' Freddy,
Over the cliff, we've got to keep the bus steady!

"Just hang on a minute, I've got an idea".
It's the end of the film, let's all go get a beer.

On days like these the film would not have been made,
It sometimes feels like we have all been betrayed.

Political Correctness, which is totally mad,
The 'M' word's taboo, fundamentally bad.

So, tell me what's left of our freedom of speech
Has it completely all gone, is it out of our reach?

Perhaps to do-gooders I sound like a prat,
But I really must say, I preferred days like that.

My Parkinson's

I received my diagnosis
In two thousand and thirteen
It was not what I expected
Was completely unforeseen.

You see, I'd just turned fifty
My life on course and set
Geriatrics just got Parkinson's
I didn't think I was one yet.

To be told that you've got Parkinson's
Is hard to bear at any age
But to hear it in your fifties
Feels like you've just caught the plague.

Now, I didn't know that Parkinson's
Was an equal opportunities employer
It affects the young and very old
It is an any age destroyer.

Continued

I didn't want to mix with others
In fact it took me five long years
I preferred to stay in isolation
I didn't want to meet my peers.

And the thing that made me change my mind
Was from Parkinson's UK
It was something in the local rag
A Parkey café's on its way.

Then I joined the local support group
Which is in my local town
They're a right good bunch of people
Volunteers form its backbone.

So, I started volunteering
You know it's really not that bad
Because I've made some super friendships
Among the best I've ever had.

I'd rather not have Parkinson's
But I have and you know what?
I won't let this bugger beat me
I'll fight it with everything I've got.

I hope they'll find a cure some day
And what a great day that'll be
The Parkinson's staff will lose their jobs
I'll gladly be their referee.

Until then, I'll make the most of it
Helped by a wholesome attitude
I hope you liked my choice of words
In my Poetic interlude.

Magic Mali

The Parkinson's Disease Society
Began in nineteen-sixty-nine
Before that there was nothing
So, it wasn't before time.

It's because poor Mali Jenkins
Couldn't find any assistance
Caring for her sister, Susan
With her Parkinson's existence.

There was no one to support them
So, she started her own group
Sixteen came to the first meeting
It must have felt like quite a scoop.

She began our well-known charity
Which gives support and good advice
The Parkinson's Disease Society
Its Sunday name to be precise.

Over time it has developed
Into what we have today
With Staff, Researchers, Volunteers
Now it's 'Team' Parkinson's UK.

Prince Philip battled sickness for several days not wanting to cause a fuss – until doctors finally persuaded him to go to hospital.

17 February 2021

Duke

His highness is in hospital,
All the news reporters tell,
Guess that's just to be expected,
When you're ninety-nine as well.

He's knocking on a bit now,
Really just a matter of time,
Before we get a day off.
Wonder what I'll do with mine?

Half Hancock'd

The definition of insanity,
As Albert Einstein said,
Is to always get the same result,
But expect a different one instead.

So poor old half-witted Hancock,
Must be really round the bend,
To admit on Andrew Marr's show,
Where his holidays he'll spend.

He mentioned it some time ago,
In Cornwall he would stay,
Which really caused an awful row,
The Cornish wished he'd stay away.

The trouble for poor Hancock,
Was when he spoke of his vacation,
We had all been told to stay at home,
A governmental proclamation.

Foreign hols became a big taboo,
As were holidays at home,
Even here in 'Bonny' Scotland,
We all had lost our 'right to roam'.

Last week he said it yet again,
On the same TV news show,
It was like a kind of Groundhog Day,
He had reached an all-time low.

He was interviewed by Andrew Marr,
Who comes across as a nice bloke,
But the answers that Matt Hancock gave,
Could give Marr a second stroke.

It seems that Matthew is determined,
To have his holiday away,
He has coughed up his deposit,
And in Cornwall he will stay.

His colleagues, they are all furious,
'Cos it's on the nation's radar,
Now they won't be going anywhere,
Either near to home or far.

But that's not for our dear Hancock,
He is so different so it seems,
Perhaps he'll even get to Cornwall,
But mostly in his dreams.

Covid has shown the power of science –
industry collaboration creates vaccine in record
time   16 June 2021

What If?

Why did I have to get this
My disorder of the brain?
Why did it have to happen?
My life will never be the same.

Out of neurological disorders
Mine is probably the best
Tell my shaking aching body that
It knows that Parkinson's a pest!

Now there is no doubt about it
Multiple Sclerosis is a curse
Huntington's disease will kill you
It really can't get any worse.

I might sound unsympathetic
But I'm not interested in those
Because it's Parkinson's that ails me
So, to that I'm predisposed.

During lockdown I was thinking
About pandemic and the cure
The way they worked to make a vaccine
That thanks to science we'll endure.

What if they all worked together
Those researching neuroscience
Maybe then they'd quickly find a cure
With their collaborative alliance?

What if all of the researchers
Shared the things that they'd discovered
They could compare their scientific notes
And then a cure could be uncovered?

There's just one major stumbling block
Who names the cure for all to see?
Because Professors have big egos
Why not just name it after me!

Alternative Valentine

Roses are red
Violets are blue
I've got Parkinson's
Thank God my carer is you.

Roses are red
Violets are blue
Happy Valentine's Day
Now go and make me a brew!

Tiger Woods car crash: Golfing great
drove at almost double the speed limit
23 February 2021

Car Crash Conundrum

Tiger Woods has crashed his car again
It's becoming quite a habit
The last time that he did it
He claimed he'd swerved to miss a rabbit

Turns out Tiger is a Buddhist
Believing everything is sacred
He'd rather crash than kill something
Especially if it is endangered

This time he took avoiding action
He didn't want to squash a toad
That was mating on the tarmac
In the middle of the road

The toads first and final warning
That their existence was in peril
Was when the male toad saw the speeding car
And shouted "Brace yourself now Beryl!"

To say that Beryl was excited
When she heard Big Bernie cry
Wasn't what she had expected
She never lived to wonder why

It's ironic that the toads were killed
While they were mating for dear life
Their species closer to extinction now
They've lost Big Bernie and his wife

And the moral of the story?
Perhaps is Tiger shouldn't drive
Or he shouldn't speed on county roads
If he wants wildlife to survive

There's another lesson to be learned
This one's for the slippery toad
You will always be endangered
If you insist on shagging in the road

Who'd A Thought It?

A year ago, give or take a day,
With Covid refusing to go away,
The Government told us all to lockdown,
And stay in bed under the eiderdown.

No one thought it would last a year,
Three sixty-five days devoid of cheer,
Except of course for our Zoom meetings,
Our new found friends with their cheery greetings.

The virtual parties that we have all had,
Trying desperately to show that we are not sad,
All clapping for the NHS,
And brave Captain Tom More, now laid to rest.

Tension abounds in the ICU,
Working flat out, so God bless the few,
This really feels like we're fighting a war,
It's the nursing staff that we're so grateful for.

And what will the history books have to say
About Government actions during the fray?
And any decisions that they might have made,
Lack of PPE and Quarantines delayed.

KEEP YOUR DISTANCE
←—2 METRES—→

Continued

There has of course been the occasional blip,
Dominic Cummings' and his Bernard Castle trip,
Boris admitting shaking hands with all,
With poor Jon Van-Tam looking on, so appalled.

Now a year has passed, further on down the line,
You'll notice that I'm still imbibing red wine,
They say on a 'school day' that you shouldn't drink,
But the odd glass or two won't matter, I think.

Now I've got to ask, 'How's your year been?'
I'll not begrudge you a loudish scream,
The second anniversary is traditionally cotton,
Don't tell me you feel that you've hit rock bottom.

Although we're not completely out of the trees,
The good news is we're not down on our knees,
We have a new vaccine that is bound to help,
Just keep yourself right, 'cos you've all been telt!

Totally Tea

There's a question I've been pondering,
It often gives me a sore head,
If Parkinson's makes me feel quite drunk,
Should I stick with lemonade instead?

Does my Parkinson's control me,
Or should I take the lead instead?
But it's made me a cheap night out,
I'd rather go back home to bed.

It seems that with this 'ere condition,
When I've had a drink or two,
I end up wanting forty winks,
When I'm not desperate for the loo.

Now the solution to this question?
Stay at home and just drink tea,
Although I'd not be woolly headed,
I'd still have an urgent need to pee!

Every Covid Has a Silver Lining.

They say there's always two sides
To every single story
But this one's made in heaven
Especially for the Tories.

The Government's saved millions
On the Old Age Pension scheme
Putting people back in nursing homes
With Covid still rife on the scene.

It's obviously the easy way
To balance out the budget
After handouts made so generously
Now they won't have to fudge it.

It's been quite a tidy windfall
They've done well from the pandemic
Won't have to raise our taxes
What a great vote winning gimmick.

Just like way back in the eighties
When the Falklands timed it right
And Maggie got a landslide
Winning wars and votes outright.

Continued

Let's not forget in twenty-ten
We had another global crisis
It wasn't a pandemic
And not to do with ISIS.

It was of course the banking crash
The Tory Party was all set
Cameron riding his white charger
With Labour's letter of regret.

"I'm afraid that there's no money left"
Said the note that Cammy showed
As he held it in his sweaty hands
The defeated government to goad.

You'll see a pattern is emerging
One we shouldn't take lying down
The Tories win elections
When a crisis comes to town.

Now is it just coincidence
Or is it down to their connections?
Perhaps they've sold their tarnished souls
And that the Devil rigs elections!

Limericks

#1

There once was a Parkinson's person
Who's decorating career was uncertain
He had a really bad stammer
Which complimented his tremor
And made his painting career take a b-b-b-burton

#2

To have Parkinson's young is a worry
Working's hard if your brain becomes blurry
Then there's shaking and freezing
Motor functions decreasing
Why not pack up and retire from work early?

Whodunnit?

Come on Megan tell the truth
'Cos now we want to know,
Clear away the steaming pile of beans
You've spilt on Oprah Winfrey's show.

Who asked about the state of play
About your unborn baby's colour?
You say it's not the Queen or Duke
And it can't be Harry's mother!

To surmise, it was his Grandad
An easy route for us to take,
It's the type of thing he's said before
It's the sort of gaff he'd make.

But you're adamant that it's not him
Are you sure that you're not wrong?
We would certainly believe it,
He's said such stuff his whole life long.

So, if it's not the dear old Duke
Then who's next on Megan's list?
It's becoming an obsession,
One that we cannot resist

It's wonderful and thank you
For the difference that you've made,
You've bumped Covid off the headlines,
The virus is at last waylaid.

Well, whoever asked the question
The palace needs a new scapegoat,
I bet they pick Prince Andrew
He's the one that gets my vote.

Medication

I sometimes tend to wonder
What my medication does to me
It feels that I've been popping pills
For an eternity.

Sorry, that's an exaggeration
I've been told a million times
Another exaggeration
I'm prone to them you'll find.

Now I take so many of these pills
It's a wonder I don't rattle
And they've got some nasty side-effects
Some you might just have to battle.

When you find the info leaflet
That's folded neatly in the box
Nestling with those blasted little pills
Do not read it - you'll be shocked.

The leaflet tells of dreaded side-effects
From mojo loss to sex addiction
Constipation, loss of bowel control
Worse than the original affliction.

There's a desperate urge to gamble
Or just to spend all of your money
You tend to nod off in the evening
Or in the garden when it's sunny.

Whichever way you look at it
You really haven't got a choice
Without your medication
Parkinson's has the loudest voice.

Duke's Last Post

The good old Duke of Edinburgh
Is resting now in peace
He has gone to meet his maker
From this life he's been released.

He's planned every single detail
Want's the funeral done his way
Even designed his own Land Rover
To bear his coffin on the day.

The only thing he hadn't planned
Was that Covid was pandemic
In Windsor Chapel sat his wife
A lonely regal geriatric.

But the night before the funeral
While the Queen was deep in mourning
Boris Johnson's at a party
So, next day he's tired and yawning.

So farewell old Duke of Edinburgh,
Or for short the Duke of Ed,
Or to make it even shorter,
You'd simply say that he is D-Ed.

World Parkinson's Day

Today is the day as the saying often goes,
World Parkinson's Day if you're not in the know,
But why the eleventh of April each year?
It's James Parkinson's birthday so, let's all give a cheer.

His life started in Shoreditch a long time ago,
The year 1755 if you really must know,
He lived sixty-nine years until his demise,
Still in Shoreditch, didn't get far, I guess you'd surmise.

Well, that's where you're wrong, you've got to be told,
He made a discovery for all to behold,
He identified the condition that was given his name,
To be true 'Shaking Palsy' sounded terribly lame.

Continued

41

What else did he do if this wasn't enough?
He kept himself busy studying fossils and rocks.
He fathered eight children with his poor darling wife,
Who couldn't say 'NO' in Victorian life.

'No more history lessons!', I heard someone say,
But that's why this date is World Parkinson's Day,
It's to celebrate what studying this disease can achieve,
So, if you've got Parkinson's don't feel too aggrieved.

Our condition is subtle or can be at first,
A shake or a shimmy can't get any worse,
But as you all know that just isn't the case,
Be it speedy or slow we are all in the race.

It is spreading so fast this neurological condition,
Almost one in five hundred suffers this imposition,
Ten million poor souls are afflicted worldwide,
That's ten million families been put off their stride.

So, what's there to celebrate, what's that all about?
We've got flipping Parkinson's, I can hear you all shout,
Well, the more that we make other people aware,
The more we inform them the more they will care.

Perhaps they'll donate a wee shekel or two,
Every penny does count in the search for a cure,
One day we'll find out what has caused this disease,
The appliance of science will bring it to its knees.

Now I don't mean Zanussi will help find a cure!
They'll keep your clothes clean of that you can be sure,
The researchers are key this conundrum to solve,
In their crisp white lab coats and their steady resolve.

Researchers should know they have one thing from us,
It's the knowledge that in them completely we trust,
They'll conquer this horrid debilitating disease,
Or at least make it so I don't pee when I sneeze!

So, let's wish Happy Birthday to Parkinson, Jim,
Because putting it simply if it wasn't for him,
We'd all have 'Shaking Palsy' or it's posh Latin name,
'Paralysis Agitans' which just don't sound the same!

Lorraine Kelly and Piers Morgan slam 'Woke Brigade' amid Snow White consent kiss row

6 May 2021

That's No WOKE

What exactly does WOKE stand for?
I'm not entirely sure,
But it sounds like such a load of tosh,
It's probably manure.

It's about social injustice
Or how things are now perceived,
The way people are being treated,
The fact that some are so aggrieved.

Well, I'm upset, I am furious
That they're picking on Snow White,
The nineteen-thirties Disney film.
What gives them the bloody right?

It's all about the prince's kiss
On Snow White in her glass coffin,
Because it wasn't done with her consent,
My mind's gone completely boggling!

They say it gives a green light,
If you aspire to be a rapist,
'Cos you watched the film when you were five,
You can tell that to your therapist.

So come on you lot and 'get a grip'
It's a Disney kids' cartoon,
We know that Minnie's fucking Goofy
Except when Mickey's in the room!

Who the hell do I complain to?
That I've got Parkinson's Disease,
Because I am so bloody furious,
Can the WOKE crowd help me please?

Mental Health Awareness Week
This year we're being invited to immerse ourselves
in the '5 Ways of Wellbeing'.

10 to 16 May 2021

Don't Do It.

I'd like to pose a question,
And the answer? You decide,
It's to do with someone's mental health,
But more precisely suicide.

Should we respect what they're attempting,
Or should we try to give advice?
If we try to talk them out of it,
Does that affect their human rights?

Or should we give them some assistance,
When they're standing on the ledge?
Or maybe give them some encouragement,
Like shove them off the flipping edge?

No! For heaven's sake don't push them,
Because then you would be arrested,
For the heinous crime of murder,
Which is hard to be contested.

If you really want to end it all,
Don't worsen rush-hour disruption,
Pick something other than a speeding train,
Take the social-conscience option.

There're so many ways to do it,
You don't have to be so mean,
You don't need to make a statement,
There's no need to cause a scene.

Don't try jumping off a building,
With loads of people down below,
You'll probably kill someone else,
Unless it's from a bungalow.

So if you want to be successful,
In your attempt at suicide,
Go away, find somewhere private,
Don't drag us into your demise.

But remember someone loves you,
It may be them that finds you dead,
Think of the trauma you'll inflict on them,
Just go get counselling instead.

'Gutted', 'Massive Blow' – Scotland fans react as
Billy Gilmour tests positive for Covid-19 missing the
crunch Euro clash against Croatia   21 June 2021

Looking Through Billy Gilmore's Eyes

Team sports during pandemic
Seems like a crazy thing to play
And football's no exception
'Cos Covid hasn't gone away.

I guess that it's all down to money
That'll be the bottom line
Because football's such big business
And money wins most any time.

Most of us have had the vaccine
And we want our old lives back
But the vaccine's not a cure-all
Some forget that, that's a fact.

Is the virus going to stay away
Or has it bought a season ticket?
Because it doesn't play by any rules
It definitely is not playing cricket.

So, when thirty-thousand football fans
All descend on Hampden Park
And celebrate a goal that's scored
Go on to party after dark.

Continued

Why are we so flabbergasted
That a player's got the bug?
When someone ever scores a goal,
They always get a great big hug.

But they're setting bad examples
For the simpler kind of folk
Who 'think that it is all over'
And Social Distancing's a joke.

Thanks to Darwin for his theory
On how we all evolved
It's the survival of the fittest
Except where football is involved.

Dial Emma

I've met this fascinating person
Who I really rather fancy
But I shouldn't phone up Emma
Because I'm going out with Nancy.

If I was to telephone her?
Maybe that would be too chancy
It wouldn't be acceptable
Because I'm going out with Nancy.

Haiku #1 to #3

Haiku is a form of Japanese verse most often composed, in English versions, of three unrhymed lines of five, seven, and five syllables.

Haiku #1

Walk in a dark wood
Stumble on a sunny glade
Spirits lifted now

Haiku #2

To say silly bull,
Is the same as syllable,
Is quite incorrect.

Haiku #3

Haiku is an art,
And it cannot be surpassed,
By other poems.

A Question Of Sorts

My consultant always asks me
On my annual appointment
Do I ever get these urges?
Is there a fly stuck in my ointment?

Do I have any compulsions?
The side effects of medication
The unlikely three amigo's
Gambling, buying and sex addiction.

Well, I never was a gambler
To lay a bet is something rash
It was never in my psyche
And I never had the cash.

And as for buying goodies
Why is that so very wrong?
I only overspend occasionally
When I rack it up on Amazon.

And as for sexual urges
Of course, they naturally occur
But my wife says she's exhausted
My restless night's the saboteur!

But whatever my condition
When the question comes my way
I reply to my consultant
That "I'm fine thanks" anyway.

1 June 2021

W.H.O.'s In A name

The World Health Organisation
Has decided on a plan
To make Covid so much more PC
Better than the Ku-Klux-Klan.

It seems that governments are anxious
That their nation gets the blame
When the virus from their area
Is a really deadly strain.

So, what's their great solution?
After all what's in a name?
If the variant is deadly
It will kill you just the same.

They have come up with a cracking plan
To help maintain a country's pride
Not a way to beat the virus
Instead, an idea that's cockeyed.

They don't think that it is fair at all
To give a strain a countries name
So, they're going to use the alphabet
So, nations cannot get the blame.

The suggestion of phonetics
Was agreed by the commission
But they really didn't think it through
It required redefinition.

Continued

Phonetics seemed like the solution
Avoiding nations stigmatised
Until the ninth type of mutation
Which means that India's despised.

And what of individuals
The Charlies, Mikes and the Romeos
Now the stigma's really personal
If Juliet's the name they chose.

So, they went into a frenzy
Needed a decision made quite quick
They didn't want the world to think
The W.H.O. was so darn thick.

Then the Turkish representative
Who was in the delegation
Suggested using the Greek alphabet
Just to piss off the Greek nation.

The committee liked the new idea
They were seeking a solution
It was just the Greeks that voted 'No'
So, they passed the resolution.

Now the Indian one's called Delta
Means there's twenty left to go
If they ever get to use Omega
We're in the shit, just goes to show!

Sign Of The Times

When Scotland's independent,
And becomes its own country,
The thing that I'll invest in?
A sign making company.

Not just a general manufacturer,
Of signs. Oh no sirree,
But the one that makes the road signs
For the reason you will see.

I've been brushing up on Gaelic,
And its usage in the past,
And there's something I've discovered,
And now a question I've to ask.

If Gaelic is an ancient language,
Now only spoken by a few.
Who is sitting there in Holyrood,
And giving Gaelic a review?

It seems that Ambulance in Gaelic,
Translates to Ambyalens instead,
Which, I guess, any old dyslexic,
Could have conjured in their head.

Continued

57

I'm quite open to suggestions,
And please correct me if I'm wrong,
But as far as I can understand,
Gaelic's quite an ancient tongue.

And in ancient times unless I'm wrong,
You couldn't dial up nine-nine-nine,
Emergency Services weren't available,
An Ambulance would take a lot of time.

So, who is doing the translations,
To bring the language up to speed?
It seems entirely pointless,
Unless Scot Gov makes a decree.

So why the waste of money,
To print both words upon the van,
When one is surely good enough?
Unless they've got a master plan.

And to make them all bilingual,
Putting both names on the sign,
Would mean it has to be much bigger,
A cunning plan and not just mine.

There's only one wee observation,
It's for the guy that writes the signs.
Google Translate says that Ambulance,
Is Carbad-eiridinn. I think you'll find.

So, when Scotland's independent,
And becomes its own country,
The thing that I'll invest in,
Is a road sign company.

Kabulshit!

I cannot watch the news tonight,
The desperation in Kabul,
We called them friends who helped us fight,
The Taliban's oppressive rule.

Now they've binned this 'old' Afghani thing,
Just forget their human rights,
Not the dream of Martin Luther King,
The stuff of nightmares every night.

It seems it was all just for nothing,
A politician's change of mind,
Signed off by presidential pen,
Our leader's deaf and dumb and blind.

While I sit here with a glass of wine,
There are people out there dying,
We've really let them down this time,
Something we've done without trying.

Afghanistan's a sinking ship,
And we're the flipping rats,
To our leaders it's a tiny blip,
And we call them diplomats?

Our politicians are myopic,
Got to find some new directions,
Climate change is 'so on topic'.
And losing wars don't win elections.

Since the 1970s, researchers believe that levodopa (a common therapy for Parkinson's disease) caused melanoma in people with Parkinson's.

Sun Foolery

By now with my experience,
You'd think I should know better,
After all, when it's a chilly day,
I always wear a woolly sweater.

But when the sun is shining bright,
And I'm out and I'm about,
I don't wear a hat upon my head,
Just what do you think of that?

Now I've heard Baz Luhrmann's record,
Suggesting people wear sunscreen,
But I forget about my baldy head,
You know exactly what I mean?

My bald patch is getting bigger,
It's growing more over the years,
Now I haven't even enough hair,
To keep the sun from off my ears.

Suppose the thing I should consider,
But more often I forget,
My Parkinson's medication,
Can have a detrimental side effect.

The leaflet says you may react,
When exposed to strong sunlight,
Skin cancer, no thanks, after all,
That just doesn't seem quite right.

So, when the sun is shining,
And is out most of the day,
And the weatherman says that it is great,
It's not going to go away.

I really must remember,
To wear a hat upon my head,
Don't want my Parkinson's physician,
Becoming an Oncologist instead!

Frightful Fitful Sleep

I haven't slept a wink tonight
Not even close to forty
I haven't even had one
Or the chance of being naughty.

The tremor in my right arm
Seems to be getting so much worse
I just can't stop it shaking
Which, is in itself an awful curse.

My tremor is so violent
It tends to make the bed vibrate
My wife has never grumbled
Although it must make her irate.

So, I get up for a milky drink
As I sip it, I feel sleepy
But my arm continues shaking
In a way it's really creepy.

It's like it's not part of my body
At least a bit I can't control
It's as if it is quite different
Even having its own soul.

And if indeed it had a soul
Then it's sold it to the Devil
Who has plagued me with my Parkinson's
On so many different levels.

I wish that God would intervene
And cast this awful daemon out
And I could then go back to bed
And get some restful sleep no doubt.

But as usual He's not listening
Even when I pray, I tend to shout
Perhaps if I believed consistently
Perhaps if I was more devout.

Continued

But that's not how he'll help me
That is never how it works
He moves in ways mysterious
He has his funny little quirks.

This thing's been sent to test me
That's what the righteous people say
Well, that's tantamount to bullying
And the bully's had his day.

So perhaps I'll turn to science
See what they can do for me instead
Perhaps it's something innovative
Like a switch inside my head.

If all my neurones form a circuit
Why can't they just switch off the power
And let me get some blessed sleep
Even if it's only for an hour.

I'm sorry I've gone on too long
This poem must now finish
But it has kept me company
When my shaking won't diminish.

I can hear my family stirring
It's the dawn of a new day
Suppose I'll just have to get on with it
My Parkinson's won't go away.

Haiku #4 to #7

Haiku # 4

Children are like farts,
You can't stand other peoples,
But relish your own.

Haiku #5

I'm feeling awful
Medication yet to work
Why the big delay?

Haiku #6

Is a syllable
Different in Japanese
To one in English?

Haiku #7

His name is Richard
Apparently prefers dick
Well, each to their own

Jigsaw Jeopardy

Support your local charity shop,
That's the message for today,
So I went and bought a jigsaw,
A thousand pieces so they say.

But there was something missing,
It nearly drove me round the bend,
There's nine hundred and ninety-nine pieces,
I only discovered at the end!

It was probably donated,
By some pseudo, do-good twat,
And they knew a piece was missing,
Just what is the point of that?

Perhaps the moral of the story,
To improve your mental health,
Give all your faulty shit to Charity,
So, they can put it on their shelf.

It will stay in circulation,
In your local charity shops,
It's in a kind of perpetual motion,
Because its journey never stops.

Instead of putting it to landfill,
You can help the habitat,
It's a win- win situation.
They'll sell it to another prat.

On A Crusade

There's an awful lot of history
Between Muslim and Infidel
With Crusaders in the Holy Land
The unbeliever hordes to quell.

Compare those times to Vietnam
Or Afghanistan today
The Middle East is still not Christian
Not by a long chalk anyway.

Nowadays we're not crusading
But preaching peace and love on earth
And we're not invading countries
In an attempt to spread the word.

Well, not for twenty years or so
When we helped the USA
Look for mass destruction weapons
A dream that hasn't gone away.

Today we don't fight for religion
Crying 'King and Country' from a steed
We want their natural resources
It's for oil our soldier's bleed.

It's the winners write the history books
To the losers' war crimes go
Should Bush and Blair be put on trial?
Win or lose, we'll never know!

Haiku #8 to #11

Haiku #8
Hens clucking nearby
Communication subtle
I'm feeling henpecked

Haiku #9
Sunlight greets my eyes
Nice to be out bathed in light
All is clear and bright

Haiku #10
Content hens bathe in dust
Inquisitively clucking
Proving they're happy

Haiku #11
Fork handle in hand
Handle for fork not candle
Nice warm cup of tea

Snow Joke

Why is everybody so surprised
To have snow in November,
Don't they know it's winter after all,
And it's right next to December?

That's the month that we all wish for it,
To be precise on just one day,
Except for William Hill or Ladbroke's,
Because then, they'd have to pay.

So, here I am with Parkinson's
People think that it's a curse
Among neurological conditions
Other types are so much worse.

'Don't let Parkinson's define you'
I've heard some people say
But it won't get any better
And it will not go away.

Of course, it will define you
It's part of everything you do
More sensible advice would be
'Don't let it take control of you'!

Take control over your Parkinson's
Attempt to get the upper hand
I've heard that exercise is excellent
Join a gym and make a stand.

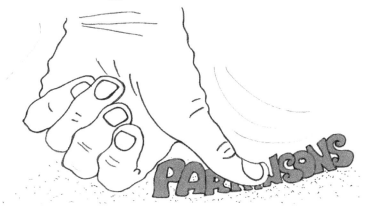

Sleaze Row is not going away anytime soon
for the Tories
16 November 2021

Tory Toerag

I can't believe what's happening,
In Parliament just now,
Right Honourable Tory members,
Treating it like a cash cow.

They're abusing their positions,
All for monetary gain,
What's the matter with these people?
Are they all devoid of shame?

They're working in Westminster,
On their second or third jobs,
And using headed notepaper,
'Cos their clients are huge snobs.

Lobbying's the money spinner,
How to make the next fast buck,
The Tory MP's rake it in,
Like they just don't give a . . . .

Just to show impartiality,
Other MP's do it too,
But the Tory's make an art of it,
Instead of working hard for you.

It's their constituents I'm sorry for,
Taken in by their charisma,
When all their MPs give them,
Is false hope like a miasma.

So, we'll let them have their second jobs,
Which they do in their own time,
But not while they're in Parliament,
Which is not their time, but mine.

Deja Who?

Are you a believer in reincarnation?
If you are - then I take it in your estimation
If I've Parkinson's, I'd been bad in past days,
In a previous life might've been Reggie Kray.

Was I Muammar Gaddafi or Saddam Hussain?
Did I throw in the towel and then hide in a drain?
Perhaps in the past I'd been Vlad the Impaler.
Or the baddie from Star Wars who needs an inhaler.

Do you believe, previously, I had been so atrocious,
That now I deserve my Parkinson's diagnosis?
Do you think that the Parkinson's people today
Must have been very bad and that's how they repay?

Had I done something that was very much worse,
For me to have picked up this Parkinsonian curse?
Been someone like Crippen or Pol Pot or Stalin,
A concept that I would no doubt find alarming.

For you to believe reincarnation applies,
I suppose that you think you are terribly wise,
You're extremely deluded is what you should know,
You get only one life 'This is not a sideshow!'

We've only one life, so give it your best shot,
If you're diagnosed, don't give up and just rot!
But if reincarnation is truly a thing,
If it is, when I come back, I'll give you a ring.

Clear Cut

Parkinson's has taught me one thing
And that's humility
It's in knowing when to give up
And let what will be, will be.

I was dining at a restaurant
With my daughter and my wife
It's my darling wifey's birthday
Forty- five again. Yeah right!

I had ordered sirloin steak this time
And it came with all the trimmings
I'd conveniently forgotten that
I was supposed to have been slimming.

This milestone in my Parkinson's
Was more subtle than I'd thought
When my 'potential carer' daughter
Noticed I was getting fraught.

She had noticed I was struggling
To cut the food upon my plate
It was not the toughness of the steak
That was making me irate.

Even though I had a steak knife
I was sorely ill equipped
Because my Parkinson's just couldn't cope
Which had not been in the script.

My daughter must have noticed
And couldn't sit and watch me suffer
So, she asked me did I need some help
Reminding me of my dear mother.

Like back when I was a toddler
And just off the baby food
Today to have my food cut up for me
I would have totally refused.

And the humility you're wondering?
Well, I accepted in a dash
I handed my plate over
The steak was diced up in a flash.

A month ago, I'd have said no
And lied that I was coping
And search for something witty
To pretend I had been joking.

So, what does all this mean for me?
Have I just given up completely?
No, unless it's a big juicy steak
I'll get it sliced and diced discreetly.

It Never Happened

I'm sorry to say,
But it happens some days,
I forget things that I've planned to do.

Once in that frame of mind,
I more often now find,
I miss what I've been looking forward to.

So please don't criticise,
When I apologise,
That I missed our planned appointment.

I recalled much too late,
That we all had a date,
When I arrived, I just found disappointment.

There was nobody there,
The room was quite bare,
Not one person was patiently waiting.

So, I quite understand,
And I'll hold up my hand,
If I'm due for some kind of berating.

So, I'm wondering now,
And to you all I avow,
I'll not miss the next date if we set one.

Let me just ascertain,
Shall we try once again?
Let me know what days suit and I'll pick one.

Boggy Trousers

I used to be quite well turned out,
Wasn't like a tailor's dummy,
Considering that I'm five foot six,
And I've a slightly bulging tummy.

I'd wear different types of trousers,
From corduroy to Harris Tweed,
As well of course my trusty jeans,
Worn depending on the need.

But now it's baggy trousers,
With an elasticated waist,
Because since I've got Parkinson's,
I don't have any time to waste.

What I mean is every second counts,
When I've got to use the toilet,
If I fumble with my trousers,
I've been sometimes known to soil it.

Usually, it's just a minor leak,
As I struggle with my flies,
But sometimes it is much, much worse,
No matter how I clench my thighs.

I've tested colours and materials,
To cover up if I've been slow,
But if you've ever filled your boots,
Then trust me, everybody knows!

So, it's good old track suit trousers,
Or 'joggy bottoms', they're for me!
Not because they pull down easily,
It's 'cos they soak up loads of pee!

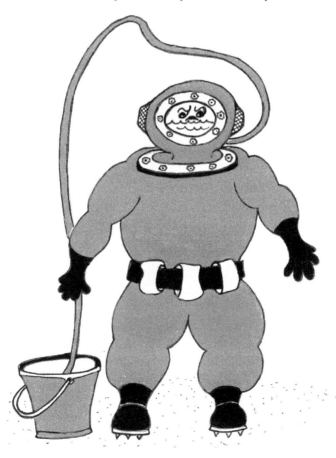

Snow Forgetting Dad

It's four-thirty in the morning,
I have had a fitful night,
I haven't really slept a wink,
As I lie here warm and tight.

It's been snowing now for ages,
The wind whipping up a storm,
When something made me think of dad,
Which wasn't usually the norm.

He had this sort of phrase he liked,
Used it with an impish grin,
Something I did not appreciate,
Which in hindsight was a sin.

It was in my bed next to my wife,
That I realised with glee,
Exactly what my dad had meant,
When he said that phrase to me.

It was while I was lying here awake,
The snow whipping past my window,
With my wife asleep right next to me,
Such a wonderful bedfellow.

I thought of the snow storm raging,
What if I was out at sea,
The best place to find shelter,
Is anchor in an island's cosy lee.

The best haven I have ever found,
Is lying sleeping next to me,
She's so kind and such a loving wife,
And I adore her completely.

And what about my father's saying?
The one that sprang to mind,
Well, I couldn't fit it in my rhyme,
So, it's below for you to find.

"There's nothing quite
like being anchored in
the lee of Titty-bum
Island!"

Dad

Cheers To The Railway!

I've had one or two libations,
At a local hostelry,
It's got tons of friendly atmosphere,
Such a splendid place to be.

We're not known to them as regulars,
It's not like we're biggish drinkers,
But the bar staff make you welcome,
And some punters are deep thinkers.

The pub isn't 'Cheers' in Boston,
But Barbara always knows your name,
Which makes you feel so flipping good,
And reinforces why you came.

So, thanks to Barbara and the team,
At the Lower Largo Railway Inn,
For serving me with real ale beer,
And sometimes a crafty gin!

Two cases of COVID-19 with mutations consist with B.1.1.529 identified in the UK.

27 November 2021

Oh, Come On! - Omicron!

Some thought that it was over,
Well, there's a new strain - Omicron,
We've woken with a hangover,
Covid's definitely not gone!

This variant is nowhere near the same,
Since it's mutated quite a lot,
Couldn't even have a normal name,
Like Frank or Jim or Sam or Dot.

South Africa's where it started,
And now it's over here as well,
Because our checkpoints are half-hearted,
Seems the country's gone to hell.

While Boris says don't wear a mask,
Nicola Sturgeon's kept the rules,
The question that we should all ask,
Is Westminster run by fools!

Christmas Message

At last, it's Christmas twenty-one,
And it's time to celebrate,
It's the birth of baby Jesus,
Who was delivered in a crate.

Not a crate, of course, a manger,
And in a stable far away,
Health and Safety regulations,
Would have frowned on that today.

There wasn't room at any inn,
And they hadn't booked online,
Which would have been a minor miracle,
Like turning water into wine.

I wonder what would happen,
If the Messiah came today,
Perhaps if he was here right now,
He'd be a migrant near Calais.

If that was indeed the outcome,
He wouldn't need a boat at all,
He could cross the English Channel,
Just by going for a stroll.

That sounds so disrespectful,
I really must apologise,
The fact is Christmas is a pantomime
And we should mourn its sad demise.

Christmas has become big business,
Helps the financial world stay healthy,
Forget about the Christmas message
Just help the "fat cats" to stay wealthy

Why do we buy so many presents?
How does that celebrate his birth?
Why don't we just get back to basics?
That's my advice, for what it's worth.

Lateral thinking

My daughter took a Covid test
Since she was feeling rather poorly
The lateral flow test showed two lines
Suggesting that she'd got it surely.

We went into a tailspin
We had things that we had planned
But now we'll have to isolate
At least that's what we understand.

We thought it would be sensible
If she had a PCR
To confirm the home done test result
And so, we set off in the car.

The nearest local testing site
Looked like a kind of no-mans-land
The place was so deserted
Worse than Custer's Final Stand.

They had trouble comprehending
That mum and dad were in the clear
And that the only test we needed
Was for our darling daughter dear.

Let's hope that it's a faulty reading
On the home style Covid test
We've only isolated for one day
It's like we're under house arrest.

They say that Covid is a killer
Well, that might indeed be true
If I'm locked up with my family
I might become a killer too!

Nichola Sturgeon blames Steps for Omicron
Covid outbreak
3 December 2021

Taking Steps

So, Omicron has just invaded
And doing well, which is annoying
Much better than the poor old Nazis
Who got no further than Boulogne.

Westminster's looking for a scapegoat
Searching for someone else to blame
Who let it come in undetected?
It always is the bleeding same.

It seems the culprit is a pop group
Who'd reformed some months ago
They'd a massive show in Scotland
At the Hydro in Glasgow.

And the pop group? Well, it's Steps of course
With their nineties throwback fans
In their polyester shell suits
Waving lighters in their hands.

It's the politicians' fault, not Steps
A 'tragedy' they got the blame
(By the way in nineteen-ninety-eight
They had a hit with the same name).

It was down to the World Leaders
And their eager hangers on
Not successful at COP twenty-six
Except to share their Omicron.

Consternation

I'm wondering can you help me
About a situation please?
Because I've already got my Parkinson's
Don't want another big disease.

It's to do with going to the toilet
Number twos to be precise
Sorry if you're eating breakfast
But I've been up half the night.

It all started with a tummy ache
And something didn't feel quite right
Because my guts were really churning
Which gave my wife an awful fright!

My toilet habit is like clockwork
Never known to be unstable
Not quite a ship's chronometer
More like a bus or train timetable.

What's the best way to describe it?
How on earth to set the scene?
Without being too explicit
But so, you know just what I mean.

Well, I get an urgent signal
That I really want to go
But after ages on the toilet seat
There's almost nothing there to show.

I can't sit like that forever
Someone else might need the loo
When the desperate urge takes over me
I'm going to jump the flipping queue.

Next time I'm more successful
With my intestinal tribulations
There's a sort of big explosion
Rocking me to my foundations.

Continued

But it seems I'm not yet finished
There is so much more to come
As my gurgling tummy testifies
It's tighter than a big bass drum.

And so, it went on through the night
And when I woke to a new day
I really hoped it was all over
And all behind me as they say.

Out of all the Parkey symptoms
Constipation is just one
Should I worry it's more serious
This large intestinal tantrum?

So please give me reassurance
Tell me that I'm not alone
Throw a drowning man a lifeline
Give this poor old dog a bone.

Shake That

My constant shake's annoying,
It's becoming quite a bore,
My wife, she used to like it,
But now it just makes her sore!

10 Dec 2021 — Covid variants are now all named after Greek letters, rather than the country they originated in

Alphabet Stew

The first letter is Alpha
In the Greek alphabet
And second is Beta.
Says my wife's pal Janette

Alpha/Beta gives the name
To what we had to learn at school
Consisting of twenty-six letters
The Alphabet recited as a rule

But it is so very different
From the old Greek composition
The letters number only twenty-four
Completely Greek to a Phoenician

The World Health Organisation
Like to flaunt their education
Naming Covid strains in Ancient Greek
They're looking for our adulation

Continued

The Met Office guys are just the same
Naming storms by alphabet
But it seems the chaps at the W.H.O
Are playing an alphabet roulette

The Met Office sticks to basics
Names each tempest in strict order
While the W.H.O. name COVID strains
As if they have been made to order

Beta follows Alpha
And then Gamma's next in line
Then Delta and then Epsilon
It's been that way for all of time

Zeta, Eta, Theta take their turn
A fact that's known by everyone
The next one is Iota
The W.H.O's not got that one

They've jumped them all with Omicron
Which is way way down the list
There's another five before it's due
The W.H.O completely missed

There are some that are a worry
With Lambada being just one
If you're infected with that kind of strain
You'll be dancing all night long!

The penultimate one's just known as PSI (Si)
The P should not be heard
Like when you're going to the toilet
Which is a metaphor absurd

The last one, of course, Omega
Which signifies the end
And if Covid was to last that long
We'll all be driven round the bend

Jane Asher

Jane Asher is the President
Of Parkinson's UK
She's not studied much neurology
But she knows loads anyway.

I saw Jane Asher recently
She hasn't changed a bit
Although she has baked loads of cakes
She's still looking rather fit!

Litigation Nation

All of those warnings make me wonder
If companies think that we're daft
Do they think we're all born yesterday
Or just arrived in a spacecraft?

They're telling us how to stay safe
Their advice we all should follow
How have we all survived till now?
You have to chew before you swallow.

Now I know a cardboard coffee cup
Contains liquid that is hot
Otherwise, I'd want a refund
Don't want cold coffee from the pot.

And I've known that peanut butter
Is made from nuts since I was four
Without nuts it's just plain butter
Which would, let's face it, be a bore.

Or a bag of rice that has been cooked
In a microwave before it pings
Will probably be scalding hot
Any idiot knows such things.

Like that eyes and soap don't mix too well
That's why we're careful when we wash
But then I realised, undoubtedly
What's behind all of this tosh.

They're not on tins and packs to help us
These so-called welfare warning signs
It's more from fear of litigation
Which is the curse of modern times.

So, it's thanks to the Americans
And their outrageous compensation
Giving cash to Darwin's losers
Is not the way of evolution.

Continued

Some law firms claim they'll help you
'No win no fee' is what it's called
Really, they're just chasing ambulances
Darwin would have been appalled!

It seems that natural selection
In the court room don't apply
Burnt by steaming hot Mac-Cherry Pie?
Then sue Macdonald's you should try.

And then a second thought occurred to me
Confirming they must think we're thick
It's those daft 'serving suggestions'
Enough to drive a man to drink!

But the note says 'drink responsibly'
As displayed on every bottle
Is it advice or a philosophy?
Wish we could ask old Aristotle!

More Limericks

#3

There once was a nurse, name of Claire,
Whose primary role in healthcare,
Was for Parkinson's folk,
Which was no flipping joke,
There's so many it made her despair!

#4

Parkinson's, ain't what you'd choose for yourself,
As if you could pick what's ails you off a shelf,
But what if you could?
What's the likelihood?
You'd choose something less crap for yourself!

Space Station

A cloudless sky and the stars are bright
The Space Station shining clear in flight
They're looking down on us, you think?
It's five past eight here, time for a drink
What time zone are they living in
In their spacecraft made of tin?
It's not on NASA time they run
But Universal Standard Time, 'By gum!'
That's Greenwich Mean Time - GMT
The Standard Time for the galaxy.

Boris defends staff over law-breaking party in No. 10 saying
they had 'worked blindingly hard for a very long time'.

15 December 2021

Taking The Piss (Up)

Now the latest revelation,
Of this year twenty-twenty-one,
Is not about the virus,
That they're now calling Omicron.

It's about a Christmas party,
Held at Number 10 last year,
It seems that while we were in lockdown,
They're having cheese and wine and beer.

As for the Covid regulations,
It seems to them they don't apply,
They make rules and they break them,
And when they're caught out, they just lie.

Politics today is simple,
Those in power do not care,
Boris does just what the hell he likes,
He doesn't even comb his hair.

Next time he's at the podium,
And he tells us there's a spike,
What should be our first reaction?
Thank you, Boris, take a hike!

Not The Christmas Present We Wanted

My lovely darling, gorgeous wife,
Received a text today,
Telling her that she's got Covid
The PCR results now say.

She received the proclamation,
About eight on Christmas morning,
While the rest of her dear family,
Were in bed and loudly snoring.

Unfortunately, it came to pass,
That darling daughter and dear me,
Booked a ten-thirty A.M. testing slot,
At the PCR facility.

It was really so efficient,
Like it was part of the army,
And in these virus laden troubled times,
That doesn't sound too flipping barmy.

It resembled all the places,
In those classic Zombie flicks,
Where you hide from all the 'Living Dead',
And shit a truck load of loose bricks.

But it wasn't a safe haven,
'Cos when we both had done our test,
We were quickly shown the way out,
With a "Thanks" and "All the best"

And the outcome of the story,
Was that we were in the clear,
Just my wife left isolating,
So much for our Christmas cheer!

Hen Pecked

There's so much more to keeping hens
Than any book will tell you
Or the 'know it all' thing internet
Or the farm that sells them to you.

They'll inform you how to give them care
From the basics how to hold them
How to keep their hen house nice and clean
But they are yours once they have sold 'em.

Just like on any new adventure
We have made the odd mistake
Realising four fresh eggs a day
Was more than our family could take.

And so, our eggy surplus
Keeps our friends and neighbours fed
We never ask for any money
Just empty egg boxes instead.

Now we haven't got a cockerel
So, the hens don't make much noise
Except when cats invade their garden
That's when they tend to lose their poise.

Then the noise is quite alarming
As they squawk and run around
It seems to be at seven thirty
On a weekend I'll be bound.

Now I got them for a purpose
So that I didn't laze in bed
And I'd like to say that it has worked
I'm up at six o'clock instead.

Really, I'm not going to egg you on
But they are so much fun to keep
They're such fascinating creatures
Well worth the weekend lack of sleep.

Predictive Cure

Seeing the funny side of Parkinson's,
Is a knack that keeps you sane,
Celebrating something crazy,
Like Gene Kelly singing in the rain!

Or the times when you are texting,
And you've a tremor in your thumb,
And the words that you have written down,
All come out completely wrong.

What if you went to correct them,
But you just left them, let them be?
Could that be your Parkey texting?
Wonder what's the possibility?

And just what would Parkey tell us,
About this Parkinson's disease?
If it monopolised your texting,
By using random words to tease.

Perhaps the words begin to take some shape,
Into a sentence that makes sense,
And that perhaps it can communicate,
Potentially this would be immense.

What if Parkey's not malevolent,
Doesn't like being a disease?
It could tell us how to find a cure,
By predictive text with ease.

So now next time that you are texting,
And you make a daft mistake,
Hang on there, don't erase it,
Just carry on for Parkey sake

2021 A To Z

Here's my A to Z of the year, Twenty Twenty-One.
If it wasn't for Covid it would have been much more fun.

A's for AstraZeneca
The vaccine for all

B stands for Boris
He's due for a fall

C is for Christmas
There's no partying here

D stands for Downing Street
And the parties hosted last year

E stands for Exercise
Or complete lack of it

F is for Face-masks
Where's yours you halfwit?

G stands for Gove
And his trendy dance move

H is for Hancock
His wife didn't approve

I stands for Idiot
That's Hancock again

J's Jason Leitch
And his amazing new fame

K is for Kiss
On Hancock's CCTV

L is for Lobbying
Patterson's money making spree

M stands for Macron
Thinks our PM's a
clown

N is for No's
Tory rebellion put
down

O stands for Omicron
Found roaming the
street

P is for President
Trump far from
discreet

Q stands for
Quizmaster
Here's Boris on Zoom

R for Reshuffle
Rayner's not in the
room

S is for Shropshire
The Lib-Dems win the
cup

T is for 'Time Please'
As the pubs all shut up

U stands for U-Turn
The standards debate

V is for Virus
Watch this bastard
mutate

W's for Windsor
Now Prince Harry's
surname

X is for Ex-Royal's
What is Megan's end-
game?

Y stands for Yorkshire
And its racist cricket
club

Z's for Zuckerberg
And his Congressional
snub

Continued

I hope you agree what a year this has been,
It was bad for us all but spare a thought for the
Queen.

Nobody knows how next year will transpire,
Will Tony Blackburn finally decide to retire?

Will a general election see the Boris lot beaten?
That shambolic scarecrow educated at Eaton

Will Indiref be forefront of Nichola's mind
Or will Eck come along and tackle her from behind?

Nobody knows and does anyone care?
Just as long as the virus can't be found anywhere!

Lisa

Lisa used to be a looker
I remember from the past
I met her just the other day
Boy, she's going downhill fast!

Catastrophe

There's a dead cat lying out in the street,
At the bottom of our road,
It's a shame but these things happen,
If you don't use the Green Cross Code.

There's no doubt it will be sorely missed,
By someone in the Crescent,
And since there's lots of traffic,
By now it won't look all that pleasant.

When you lose a much-loved pussy,
It always is a crying shame,
But this one can be easily found,
'Cos it's decomposing in the drain.

Boris Johnson apologises for No. 10 party & US
Judge decrees Prince Andrew must attend
hearing in the States   12 January 2022

Party Poopers

Boris Johnson has admitted it
He was at a 'do' in lockdown
But since we know that he's a liar
Can he survive this latest knock down?

You can always tell he's is lying
Because that's when he moves his lips
Suppose that now it doesn't matter
Seems either way he's had his chips.

The bigwigs of the Tory Party
Have the knives out all prepared
At least he'll go with quality
They're solid silver. If you cared?

116

The next one that's been caught at it
Is Prince Andrew, Duke of York
All the girls know that he sweats a lot
Just before he pops his cork.

News just in! He'll have to go to court
And stand before a US Judge
But since the War of Independence
The Royals have held a massive grudge.

To them it's still a colony
Therefore, has no jurisdiction
He can't stand in a U.S. court
While they judge his girl addiction.

He's becoming an embarrassment
The Queen's second eldest son
He could always go with dignity
Could someone please give him a gun.

Or he could take his cue from Harry
And go and live out in LA
Doesn't need a crib in Beverley Hills
With his pal Maxwell he'll stay.

HRH U Turn

I'm feel quite sorry for Prince Andrew,
I understand why he's irate,
Now he's just lost all his privileges,
Because a girlfriend was jailbait.

You couldn't blame him in his twenties,
When a girl came onto him,
He didn't ascertain her date of birth,
Or does she use a pseudonym?

I'd just count myself as lucky,
If such a young girl fancied me,
And I wouldn't stop to question her,
At what is now a great party.

And then I bet he can't believe it,
She's flown across the wide Atlantic,
So that she could go to bed with him,
To ask her age would be pedantic.

Now when he sees her in that photo,
Looking so much older than her age,
And she's drinking booze and putting out,
No wonder he's outraged.

Haiku #12 to #14

Haiku #12
Sweat on lip salty,
Too much done I shouldn't sweat,
Good to be active.

Haiku #13
Wet leaves are warming,
Croci bathing in the sun,
Musty earth is turned.

Haiku #14
The garden neater,
Pots brimming on patio,
Wallet empty now!

Enjoy Your Trip

With Parkinson's my gait's unsteady,
A walking stick? I'm not yet ready.

Instead, I tend to shuffle along,
Which for my age is totally wrong.

'Cos then I look like an old codger,
Instead of being the Artful Dodger.

It seems my feet are made of clay,
Not porcelain not anyway.

I'll sometimes sway and trip and fall,
I look quite drunk but not at all.

It's Parkinson's done this to me,
Not alcohol, not totally.

So, if you see me on my back,
I haven't had a heart attack.

And neither am I roaring drunk,
That is a myth I must debunk.

Instead, I simply tripped and fell,
End of, there is no more to tell.

Expect if I had used a stick,
I'd not lie here looking like a dick!

5G or not 5G

I've purchased a new mobile
And its network is 5G
So, it's got a stronger signal
That's what the salesman said to me.

In fact, the signal is so flipping strong
That even when I'm on a flight
I can use my brand-new mobile
Which I soon discovered wasn't bright.

It was late on I remembered
As the plane fell like a stone
That in the cabin crew announcement
They mentioned not to use your phone.

It seems that aircraft guidance systems
Get interference from 5G
So, take heed of pre-flight briefings
Don't use your 5G phone like me.

Now if it's any consolation
The 5G signal was so good
That the person I was calling
Could hear my screams and understood.

And the last thing that I heard them say
Before we ploughed into the ground
Was "I bet some twat's on 5G"
Which was really quite profound.

Birthday Blowout

In the PM's party scandals
Was his birthday celebration
When he blew out all the candles

They all wished him Happy Birthday
And then they all broke into song
Their consensus of opinion
Was that they could do no wrong

They didn't heed the regulations
That they'd imposed on all of us
Or if they did, they just ignored them
And wonder why we make a fuss?

It seems as leader of the country
Boris doesn't seem to be that bright
Thought they were singing Happy Birthday
So his hand washing was timed right

It makes me want to pose the question
Why's he's still in Number Ten
Can't trust him to do anything
Even winding up Big Ben

Just a minor point of order
Big Ben's the nickname for the bell
In the Elizabethan Tower
As any guide book's sure to tell

Are We There Yet?

So, we're almost back to normal,
Restrictions lifting without strings,
But Covid's not quite down and out,
Not until that fat girl sings.

I know I shouldn't say that,
Politically Correct I know it's not,
But we have the luxury of free speech,
At least we think that's what we've got.

Over sensitive do gooders,
Would tend to strongly disagree,
Naturally they are within their rights,
Sometimes even I can be PC.

We know of that singing lady,
And we're well aware she's fat,
There you see I've said it yet again,
Because you can't avoid a fact.

To say that it's not over
Until the fat lady starts to sing,
Means she better go and warm up,
Enter stage right, do her thing.

But what if she's got Covid,
Ends up in an ICU,
And she's trying to suck in oxygen,
She'll not sing for me and you.

If she won't be blasting out her song,
We'll have pandemic without end,
So, we must find a solution fast,
Before it drives us round the bend.

Why does it have to be a woman,
Who is morbidly obese?
Choose from any fat male tenor,
There are quite a few of these.

Not Luciano Pavarotti,
Because this one's already dead.
We'll have to find another one,
Plácido Domingo'll do instead

FERRY giant P&O sparked outrage by sacking 800 staff in a video call – and replacing them with cheaper agency workers   18 March 2022

P&NO

I used to work for P&O
Cross Channel ferry to and fro
That's where I met my darling wife
Enjoyed the work, 'That was the life'.

But good things always end, they say
And good times tend to slip away
The company was so mismanaged
Its trading was severely damaged.

P&O in years gone by
Known from sunny Cape Town to Shanghai
Its reputation was sublime
The best of any shipping line.

But standards fell and shortcuts taken
Its reputation was forsaken
To make more money was their creed
To satisfy shareholder's greed.

The crew were made to live onboard
No if's or but's 'You have been told'
Accept the changes they abhorred
If they refused, they're shown the door.

No longer were the vessels cruising
Their ships all crammed with punters boozing
And crossing just to buy cheap beer
And fags and wine in Calais near.

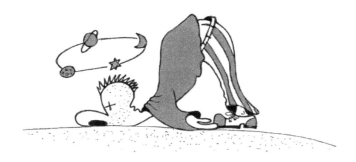

Well, that was eighteen years ago
And nothing's changed, just goes to show
The management is still so rotten
There's no respect, they've hit rock bottom.

They've sacked eight hundred - All the crew
Discarding them, they wade on through
They're being replaced by foreign labour
Bought at cut price, beggar-thy-neighbour.

They've tied the ships up to the quay
Just to compound their misery.
The replacement crew's waiting ashore.
The Merchant Navy is no more.

Continued

Consider we're an island nation
How come we're in this situation?
Ship owner's rampant greed's to blame
The history books will tell the tale

From the 'Old Man' to Galley Boy
Now on the beach and unemployed
Thank management for your demise
Bet they can't look you in the eyes.

And if you want to get afloat
Don't get on any ferry boat
This may sound like it is sedition
Please pick P&O's competition!

Starter For 16,425 Days

A momentous occasion for *(Insert your names here)*,
We are gathered today celebrating with cheer,
For forty-five years they've been in wedded bliss,
Unless you tell me, is there something I've missed?!

No seriously folks, that amounts to a lifetime,
You'd get far less in jail for a murder or drug crime,
They're a wonderful couple such a pair to behold,
He's one lucky man and he's got to be told.

(Insert her name here) did well picking this guy,
If she was playing darts, she'd have hit a bullseye.
Their biggest achievement is their lovely children,
Who might even visit if they were left half a million,

They may be quite old but they're not past it yet.
There'll be more celebrations on that you can bet.
What I really must do, wish them all of the best.
Share your secret with us so we can all pass the test.

Perfidious Albion

GB's not trustworthy, that's our reputation
Britain's not great, we're despised as a nation.

'Perfidious Albion' is what we are called
Untrustworthy in Latin, should we be so appalled?

It's how we're referred to by countries and states,
If they're fed up with us and they're feeling irate.

Cynically diplomatic not that it's any use,
To be really quite frank, we deserve the abuse.

Untrustworthy and deceitful perfidious means,
Albion refers to our old Kings and Queens.

It seems in times past we've gone back on our word,
Or diplomatically put subsequently demurred.

If someone came up with a much better deal,
The signed, sealed and ratified one was repealed.

To cover it up we've been known to start wars,
Which the rest of the world would completely abhor.

Nothing has altered going back through the years,
The spots on a leopard cannot change it appears.

Just look at this Brexit and all it entails,
No wonder the country's going right off the rails.

We have hit the buffers and carried on going,
Agreements all broke, they weren't even worth
knowing.

How can the government flout international law?
I'm pretty damn sure that's not what I voted for.

Hard boarders or soft what are we gonna do?
The country's been shafted and by only the few.

The Westminster elite have sold us down the river,
We're a branch that's been cut from the tree left to
wither.

It's reassuring our leaders are consistent, you see,
They've lied and they've cheated throughout history.

New smartwatch has potential to enhance personalized Parkinson's care.

19 April 2022

Watch it or What Shit?

They say that nine times out of ten
With Parkinson's you've a tremor
Or perhaps it's only eight, but then
That's hardly a dilemma!

There are things that make me worry
About the Parkinson's I've got
Things that make my brain go blurry
Which tends to happen quite a lot

So, to monitor my symptoms
And to get my house in order
I bought myself a 'Smart' Watch
On the internet, mail order.

But is it really such a smart watch?
What a conundrum as you'll see
Because when I put it on my wrist
It couldn't cope with my Parkey.

You see it's got these little widgets
That monitor body functions
They count your steps and heart rate
Your sleep patterns and dysfunctions.

But they're really not that clever
With my Parkinson's it struggles
The vibration of my shaking wrist
Gives false readings as it shuggles.

My tremor gets my watch confused
Thinks my heart rate is bizarre
It's so smart it calls the hospital
Who send a Paramedic in a car!

And when it comes to finger swiping
The interactive touch watch face
My shaky finger fucks it up
And puts me in a cycle race!

So does anybody want to buy
This not so clever watch of mine?
'Cos it cannot deal with Parkinson's
While I get along with it just fine ……..

…………..Mostly

Priti Awful

What on earth was Boris thinking
When he hired Priti Patel?
Was it for her warm compassion?
Go on Boris, please do tell.

Was her brief to keep our country
Completely immigration free?
To keep out all those 'Foreign Johnnies'
Who'd bring our country to its knees.

Because they hoover up the benefits
That rightfully belong to us
Or take all our really shitty jobs
Like picking fruit or drive a bus.

It's amazing how forgetful
Good old Priti is these days
Because her parents were both immigrants
From Uganda, so it says.

They came here in the sixties
They had nowhere else to go
Even though they were both Indian
Suppose it only goes to show!

Darling Priti I've got news for you
Don't you know that war is raging
And Ukraine is in an awful stew
What with Russia now invading?

Don't you know there's people suffering
That they're fleeing for their lives
From tanks and bombs and missiles?
They're just trying to survive.

Yet the brilliant British Government
Makes it hard to cross the border
Where's the visa in their passports?
Their paperwork is not in order!

Well, what on earth do you expect?
What would be your first reaction
If a tank came down your Essex street
Apply for visas your first action?

When their homes are turned to rubble
And they cannot get support
Show compassion my dear Priti
The UK is their last resort.

Continued

You can see on their faces
They would rather be at home
But their world has just been pulverised
As the nightly news has shown.

Priti pull your flipping finger out
Have you learnt nothing from Kabul?
And what's this about Rwanda?
Let them in you bloody fool!

No Rest For The Wicked

There's no rest for the wicked
Is a phrase some people use
They're obviously the lucky ones
Sleeping deeply while I snooze.

Now I know I've not been wicked
Not in this life anyway
It was not for want of trying
The chance just never came my way.

If I was wicked in a past life
Why am I paying for it now?
It shouldn't just roll over
It should be paid in full somehow.

So, the next time someone says to me
That I was bad in a past life
I'll try for some consistency
And stab them with a carving knife.

Look what lack of sleep can do to you
It can make you quite short tempered
So, please think before you say that phrase
Or you might end up dismembered!

Get It In Gretna

I'm a fully paid-up member
Of Dignity in Dying
It's down to you to choose the time
Of your demise there's no denying

If your practitioner's prognosis
Is a slow and painful death
Why put off what is inevitable
Chose when to take your final breath

There's lots and lots of people
Who have the same belief as me
Eighty five percent in Scotland
Want the law changed radically

It appears that down in England
People do not seem so keen
So, if Scotland's independent
A business opportunity I've seen

When Scotland's independent
They'll apply the public vote
You won't have to go to Switzerland
And leave behind a farewell note

You won't have to board an aeroplane
You can come to Gretna Green
We'll fulfil all of your wishes
Make your passing like a dream

Gretna Green's the destination
Flying to Switzerland's so drastic
Getting ripped off by Swiss clinics
Just come to us and flash the plastic

If it's climate change you care about.
There's no need to fly to die
'Cos we're going Green in Gretna
You'll be convinced it's a good buy.

And to prove our Green credentials
We will even plant a tree
Of course it's not a mighty Oak
But a Scot's Pine naturally.

We'll bring you across the border
If your passport is in date
We can help you die with dignity
And send you back south by road freight.

Get It On Time

Now I know there's others like me
Who don't take their meds on time
I didn't think it was a biggie
I didn't count it as a crime.

I've just come from my appointment
With my PD Specialist Nurse
She explained in words so simple
Why my Parkinson's is worse.

Her explanation made me realise
I was acting like a chump
That I wasn't being clever
Brought me earthbound with a bump.

I'm not doing me a favour
If I don't give my meds a chance
My Parkinson's I'll not control
I may as well be in a trance.

You've got to take your meds on time
So that they can work their magic
If they don't get the chance to work
The consequence could well be tragic.

They can't assess the situation
If you don't timely take your pills
Is your Parkinson's progressing?
How can your doctor treat your ills?

That's how she explained it to me
My wonderful parkinsonian nurse
So I'd better take my pills on time
Or she's really going to curse!

Dumb-roaming

It's the nanny state we've got to thank
That's encouraged simpletons to thrive
And create an idiot generation
Who need instructions to survive.

Instead of Darwin's well-known theory
Where the fuds all came a cropper
They're taking over the asylum
Fucking up genetics good and proper.

An example was the Tufty Club
Which became the Green Cross Code
If you're too daft to take their good advice
You'd end up dying in the road.

Thanks to good old nanny government
And health and safety gone too far
Even raving loons can cross a road
And not be mown down by a car.

They only have to press a button
And wait until it's safe to cross
Don't have to stop and look and listen
Without a green man they'd be lost.

And the proof that they are idiots
Is that they always stand and wait
Seems they're only waiting for my car
Which makes me so fucking irate.

When the green man says they're good to go
They'll saunter slowly across the road
And sometimes look your way and wave at you
While you just sit there and implode.

Table Tennis Talents

The latest craze for Parkinson's
That's good for fighting the condition
Helps you forget about your tremor
And leads to good coordination.

What is this new phenomenon
That's on everybody's lips?
You'd be surprised to hear it's ping pong
They've just had the UK championships.

The Second National Championships
For Parkinson's has just occurred
Even though they found it difficult
Not one of them would be deterred.

All of the players have got Parkinson's
Some more afflicted than the other
But boy those Parkey people play
As if they hadn't any bother.

The medals and the prizes
Were given out to those who won
But it's the taking part that really counts
And also having lots of fun.

They say that standing on the podium
You have a very mixed reaction
The person who received the gold
Smugly stands with satisfaction.

The one who qualified for bronze
Who obviously just scraped in third
Is elated that they've made it
Standing on the shoulders of the herd.

But the one that got the silver
Could easily have been a winner
Still thinking of the point they dropped
And now feel worse than any sinner.

Continued

Well just look upon the bright side
You ping pong playing Parkey guys
Since the condition is degenerative
This year's winner might not thrive.

If their condition has deteriorated
While your own wellbeing has not
They won't be on the podium
You'll relieve them of their slot!

So, it's good if you've got Parkinson's
And you're in an annual competition
You only need to keep the status quo
To beat the last year's opposition.

Too Depressing?

I do not want to be a burden
I do not want to take up time
I thought that I controlled my Parkinson's
It seems control is his not mine.

The Tory Faithful pick Liz Truss to be our next
Prime Minister.

5 September 2022

In God We Truss

Who would ever have believed it
Our Prime Minister's Liz Truss
She couldn't even run a bath
Now the pigeon drives the bus.

Like Mr Fraser in Dad's Army says
It appears we are all doomed
The idiot's running the asylum
Normal service not resumed.

It's alarming and a worry
That's the best the Tories got
They're pinning all their hopes on her
Now watch the country go to pot.

She didn't win an election
She don't deserve the prize
I wonder just how long she'll last
Before the voters realise!

Lean And Green

There's a very touchy subject
Which is never talked about
It's a major cause of climate change
Of that there is no doubt.

It's not meant to be offensive
But it's plain for all to see
That people who are overweight
Cause the climate catastrophe.

It's the fact that they are so rotund
It's the dimension of their girth
That's putting pressure on the planet
Third rock from the Sun, our Earth.

One of the things about a fatty
That's had a knock-on type effect
Is their clothes are so much bigger
Need more material as you'd expect.

The fact they're overeating
With their massive portion size
Means the farmers have to make more food
With the consequences that arise.

It takes more fuel to lift an aeroplane
Full of fat people off the ground
Than if the passengers were thinner
Not throwing all their weight around.

It's been said obesity's a killer
But not exclusively to fatties
Because the planet's started suffering
So now we've all had our chapattis.

Summer Frost

You would think that I would know by now
And come to terms with my condition
That my Parkinson's will not improve
I'll not experience remission

I've been lucky for ten years or so
My symptoms haven't got much worse
But it sort of just creeps up on you
In fits and starts and little bursts

I think I've started freezing more
My foot won't don its shoe
It won't obey my orders
It's like it has to think it through

An errant foot is bad enough
But now my legs have joined his gang
And my fingers strike in sympathy
As if they're on the picket line

We had a day out in St Andrews
Went window shopping, had a meal
But my body had its own ideas
And thought of ways to spike the deal

And so it started on a go slow
At least it didn't go on strike
But it started getting difficult
Because that's what Parkinson's is like

And the straw that broke my Parkey back
Was the awful revelation
That I was frozen like a statue
In the Gent's at the Bus Station

Now I must have been there quite some time
Because my wife was getting worried
And she peered around the toilet door
And found me standing there unhurried

But the thing that really got to me
The thing that made me so distressed
Was the vision of my future
How my condition had progressed.

Frozen Hot Dog

I've got a dog that's six years old
In dog years forty-two
In human years you're in your prime
And my dog feels that way too

Some dogs sniff out diseases
I think that Parkinson's among 'em
But my dog, he does it differently
My dog is definitely a wrong un

Instead of looking after me
Like a guide dog for the blind
My dog gets hot and randy
And tries to mount me from behind

It must know that I've got Parkinson's
And anticipates my freezing
'Cos when I stop inside a doorway
My extended leg it's keen on seizing

Having Parkinson's is bad enough
But to be a dog's sex toy
When I freeze and cannot move my leg
Is something I do not enjoy

So, I'm taking my dog to the vet
Not to have the thing put down
But to give his claws a right good clip
So, he won't scratch me next time round

What is Parkinson's?

Parkinson's disease is the fastest growing neurodegenerative condition in the world. Around 10 million people live with Parkinson's worldwide. Currently 145,000 people in the UK are living with the condition. With population growth and ageing, they estimate this will increase by nearly a fifth to 172,000 by 2030. Approximately 1 in every 37 people will be diagnosed with the condition in their lifetime. Every hour, two people in the UK are told they have Parkinson's.

Parkinson's not only affects those with the condition but also has a significant impact on family, friends and carers. While the majority of people develop symptoms after the age of 65, thousands of working age people are also affected. There are over 40 symptoms of Parkinson's and these can include freezing, tremor and painful muscle cramps. Parkinson's impacts mood and motivation, your ability to speak, swallow, sleep and smile. From balance to bladder control, posture and pain, Parkinson's is a full mind and body experience.

Thanks to the generosity of the public, Parkinson's UK is pouring money into research. It is leading a global collaboration with over 60 international partners who have invested over £100m in vital research. This has already delivered ground breaking discoveries, new medications and better care for those affected by this condition.

Poems In Alphabetical Order   Page No.

Other books by the author:

Reflections
Poetic Thoughts About Parkinson's, Pandemic & Life
ISBN: 978-1-5272-9012-9
Published 2021

Reflections
Poetic Thoughts About Parkinson's, Pandemic & Life
(Second Edition)
Paperback ISBN: 978-1-7393886-2-1
eBook ISBN: 978-1-7393886-3-8
Published 2023

Ingram Content Group UK Ltd.
Milton Keynes UK
UKHW022011160623
423544UK00012B/265